Hot

and

Sit on Sid

'Hot Sun' and 'Sit on Sid'
An original concept by Elizabeth Dale
© Elizabeth Dale 2023

Illustrated by Claudio Cerri (Beehive Illustration)

Published by MAVERICK ARTS PUBLISHING LTD

Studio 11, City Business Centre, 6 Brighton Road,

Horsham, West Sussex, RH13 5BB

© Maverick Arts Publishing Limited February 2023

+44 (0)1403 256941

A CIP catalogue record for this book is available at the British Library.

ISBN 978-1-84886-923-3

Maverick
publishing

www.maverickbooks.co.uk

Pink

This book is rated as: Pink Band (Guided Reading)
It follows the requirements for Phase 2 phonics.
Most words are decodable, and any non-decodable words are familiar,
supported by the context and/or represented in the artwork.

Hot Sun

and

Sit on Sid

By **Elizabeth Dale**

Illustrated by
Claudio Cerri

The Letter T

Trace the lower and upper case letter with a finger. Sound out the letter.

*Down,
lift,
cross*

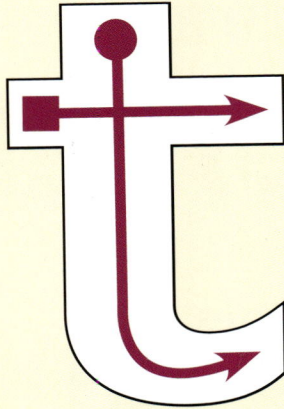

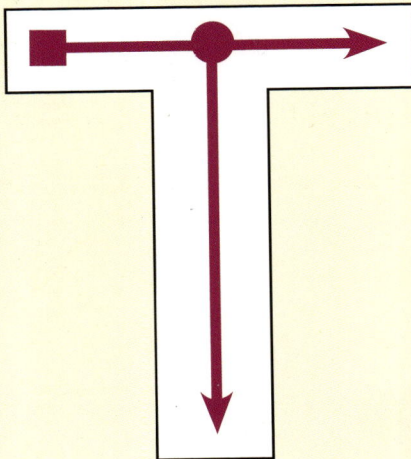

*Down,
lift,
cross*

Some words to familiarise:

sun

Ted

Bess

High-frequency words:

in   the   it   is

Tips for Reading 'Hot Sun'

- Practise the words listed above before reading the story.

- If the reader struggles with any of the other words, ask them to look for sounds they know in the word. Encourage them to sound out the words and help them read the words if necessary.

- After reading the story, ask the reader how the animals kept cool.

Fun Activity

Make fun shapes with your shadow!

Hot Sun

Pip sits in the sun.
It is hot.

Ted sits in the sun.
It is hot.

Sid sits in the sun.
It is hot.

Bess sits in the sun.
Pip is not hot.
Ted is not hot.

Sid is not hot.

But Bess is hot!

Bess is not hot!

The Letter S

Trace the lower and upper case letter with a finger. Sound out the letter.

Around, around

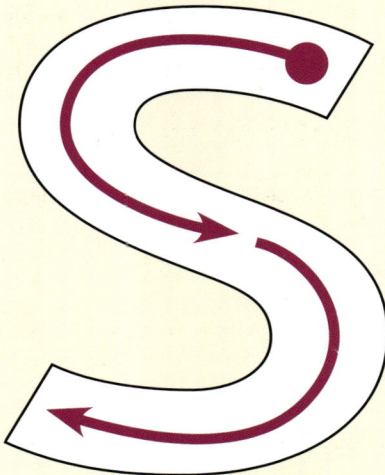

Around, around

Some words to familiarise:

Sid

Tig

rug

High-frequency words:

on   of   the   is   no

Tips for Reading 'Sit on Sid'

- Practise the words listed above before reading the story.

- If the reader struggles with any of the other words, ask them to look for sounds they know in the word. Encourage them to sound out the words and help them read the words if necessary.

- After reading the story, ask the reader why the animals fell over.

Fun Activity

Make a tower with your toys!

Sit on Sid

Pip sits on top of Sid.

Ted sits on top of Pip.

Um...

Tig sits on top of Ted.

Um...

Bess sits on top of Tig.

No, Bess!

Um...

27

Sid, Pip, Ted, Tig and Bess
sit on the rug!

Book Bands for Guided Reading

The Institute of Education book banding system is a scale of colours that reflects the various levels of reading difficulty. The bands are assigned by taking into account the content, the language style, the layout and phonics. Word, phrase and sentence level work is also taken into consideration.

Maverick Early Readers are a bright, attractive range of books covering the pink to white bands. All of these books have been book banded for guided reading to the industry standard and edited by a leading educational consultant.

Pink

Red

Yellow

Blue

Green

Orange

Turquoise

Purple

Gold

White

Cool Duck and Lots of Hats

Catch It, Jess! and Cat Nap

The Space Race

Pirates Don't Drive Diggers

A Right Royal Mess

To view the whole Maverick Readers scheme, visit our website at www.maverickearlyreaders.com

Or scan the QR code above to view our scheme instantly!